A

Himalayan

Christmas

and 'how to do a Christmas program'

Stanley Scism

Wonderful Words

iUniverse, Inc.

New York   Bloomington

A Himalayan Christmas

iUniverse books may be ordered through booksellers or by contacting:

iUniverse
1663 Liberty Drive
Bloomington, IN 47403
www.iuniverse.com
1-800-Authors (1-800-288-4677)

ISBN: 978-1-4401-7410-0 (sc)
ISBN: 978-1-4401-7411-7 (ebk)

Printed in the United States of America

iUniverse rev. date: 8/25/2010

inspired by Charles Schulz` `Peanuts` comic strip. What if he had visited the Himalayas, learned some Nepali and Hindi vocabulary, and written a Christmas special set among those lovely people? Maybe it would have been something like this.

`How to Do a Christmas Program`

Wonderful Words
L-2 Green Park Main
New Delhi 110016, India

www.wonderfulwords.us

www.stanleyscism.com

www.scismchristianuniversity.com

Dedicated to Audrene Scism, who, by answering all my questions and showing good humor, put in my heart a love of drama and learning

Dramatis Personae (first performance):

Role	Actor/Actress
Raj	Thomas Reang

and

Shanti	Charlene Shang

are brother and sister

Lalita	Christina Thapa

and

Laxman	Phillip Sailo

are sister and brother

Bara Bandar	Gopal Rai

is Raj's pet monkey

Brother Bandar	Gopal Rai

is Bara Bandar's Brother
(try to say that fast).

Anita	Rebekah Rai

and

Manoj	Benjamin Basumatary

are sister and brother

Mamtha	Susma Thapa

and

Priya	Asang Quinker

are best friends.

Raj likes 'the little Punjabi girl' (who never appears onstage), Shanti likes Laxman, Lalita likes Manoj, Laxman likes Mamtha. These infatuations are not reciprocated, yet most people have a good time.

Act 1: PRE

Scene 1: Outdoor in front of Raj's house

Raj: (sees Manoj enter and walk by carrying three signs, saying, respectively, 'only six more days until Ravi Shankar's birthday', 'eleven days until the first day of winter', 'only twelve more shopping days until Christmas'). **Rare to see one agency with all three accounts** (Manoj exits, Raj exits into his house)

Laxman (enters, faces audience): **This is my favorite time of year—I think.** (Goes to Raj's door, knocks, Shanti opens) **Trick or treat.**

Shanti: Trick or treat? This isn't Halloween (she comes out of house). **Don't you know what month this is? Don't you have a calendar?**

Laxman: I'm just an achha bachha. I don't know how to read a calendar. I don't even know what day this is. Nobody tells me anything.

Shanti: (steps back inside, then exits, then re-enters, tossing him a candy bar) **All right, here's a candy bar. Happy Halloween.**

Laxman: Thank you.

Shanti: By the way, just so you know: Today is Mother's Day.

Laxman: It is? How many days 'til Christmas?

Scene 2: Lalita's house

Lalita: (carrying a book copy of 'A Visit to St. Nicholas', to Laxman) **I feel different this year, like I have more of the real spirit of Christmas than ever before.**

Laxman: Didi, why do you suppose that is?

1

Lalita: (savagely) **BECAUSE I SAID SO, THAT'S WHY!** (He exits hurriedly)

(to Bara Bandar) **I just read this book called 'A Visit to St Nicholas'. You should make a dance from that.**

Bara Bandar: (dancing)
'Twas the year before Christmas
and all through the residence,
not a creature was stirring,
not even a president.
'Twas the month before Christmas,
and all through the school,
not a student was stirring,
not even this fool (waltzes off).

Scene 3: School

Shanti: (standing in front of class) **This is my report on how Mahatma Gandhi invented Christmas.**

Teacher: He didn't.

Shanti: (to teacher) **No?** (to class) **Boy, that kind of shoots a big hole in my report, doesn't it? I mean, like wow! Like, weird! I mean, like, where do we go from here?**

Teacher: To your desk is where you go from here.

Shanti: Yes, mem sahib.

Priya: Mem sahib, will you let us make some paper chains for our classroom Christmas tree as a class project? We could start with my math paper (holds it up).

Teacher: No, thanks.

Priya: Mem sahib? Do I understand correctly? You want us to read a book during Christmas holiday? A real book? A whole book? You're just kidding, right? Sure, you are!

Teacher: I'm not.

Priya: You *must* be!

Teacher: I'm *not*.

Priya: (slumps back in chair) **Happy holidays!** (a thought occurs) **Mem sahib, is it an interesting book?**

Teacher: That's for me to know and you to find out.

Priya: (to audience) **I hate it when she says that.** (to teacher) **I have a suggestion, mem sahib. You know what would make a perfect gift to your class? Don't assign us a book to read during Christmas holiday? How about it?**

Teacher: Even your suggestions are simple pass.

Scene 4: Raj's house

Priya: (on stage left, on phone to Raj) **Guess what? Our teacher wants us to read a book during Christmas holidays. Any suggestions?**

Raj: (who is at stage right, both characters isolated by lights) **On what book to read?**

Priya: **No, on how to escape it.**

Raj: **No.** (hangs up)

Shanti: (to Raj) **Bhaia, I also have to read a book during Christmas holiday.**

Raj: **Behena, try this one** (hands book over). **It's a real page-turner.**

Shanti: **I hate turning pages.**

Raj: **OK, I'll read your book for you. Then what do I do?**

Shanti: Then you write the report.

Raj: I hope you appreciate all this.

Shanti: I'll send you a Christmas card.

Scene 5: Outdoors

Manoj (leading trekking party): **The weather might get worse, men. Is anyone worried? Do you all know how to act in a blizzard? Does anyone have a question about anything?**

Trekker 1: Is there a place around here where we can post Christmas cards?

Manoj: (shakes his head)

Trekker 2: Have you met Sonia Gandhi? (Manoj nods) **Is she nice?** (Manoj nods)

Trekker 3: How many more shopping days until Christmas?

Manoj: Uh, I guess about thirteen. Any more questions?

Trekker 4: Why am I standing here in a blizzard with these idiots?

Manoj: (turns, starts trek again) **I didn't think I was ever going to get a sensible question** (they exit)

Scene 6: Raj's house

Raj: (playing hopscotch). **Your turn.** (she pauses) **What's the matter?**

Shanti: Listen!

Raj: What is it?

Shanti: I thought I heard something on the roof. (runs to window, looks up) **Santa Claus?**

Raj: (following her) **Reindeer?**

Shanti: Can you see anything, bhaia?

Raj: No, behena, it's too dark. Besides, it's starting to snow again.

Shanti: Do you really think it could be Santa Claus and his reindeer?

Raj: Why not? Who else?

Manoj: (to trekkers, crossing front) **I hate to admit it, but I think we're lost again.**

Scene 7: North Pole

Manoj: Elves! The place is full of them! There's the fat guy with a red suit. Let me down, men, I have a great idea (they let him fall). **That wasn't it.** (he gets up, followed by trekkers, looks over audience' heads). **I knew it! There's the sleigh. This fat guy in the red suit flies all over the world. We just hitch a ride on back, and we'll be home in no time.**

Trekker 1: Will they show a movie on this flight? (they exit off, tiptoeing).

Scene 8: Raj's house

Shanti: (to Raj) **Where's our big candy cane? It was by the tree. Now it's gone.**

Raj: Have you looked outside?

Shanti: Why outside?

Raj: Just look outside. (she does. Bara Bandar comes dancing by, with hat and using cane, stop, looks at audience).

Bara: I wanted to participate in the winter Olympics, so I started trekking. But there was this ocean, see, so I came back. So, don't worry, 'I'll be Home For Christmas.' (then pretends he's lame, uses cane to limp) **Christmas is for the innocent** (continues to limp toward exit) **I'm as innocent as can be** (shrugs) **or as possible** (limps out).

Act 2   Decorations

Scene 1: Outdoors in front of Raj's house

Raj: (in forest, to Bara) **One of life's great joys is going out into the forest and cutting down your own Christmas tree.** (they stop at one; look WAY up, Raj tries to encircle his arms around it, without success) **No sense in cutting down the first one you see. Besides, it'll never fit inside the house.**

Bara: Who cares? Let it stick out the window. I love tall trees.

Shanti: (in house, to Lalita) **Raj and Bara went out to cut down a Christmas tree.**

Lalita: That's stupid! Don't they know you can't just go out and start cutting down trees?

Shanti: Why not? Who's going to care?

Raj: (coming back to house, with Bara, both looking beat up) **I didn't know squirrels could get so upset**

Shanti: I'll go and fall down a Christmas tree.

Raj: You mean cut down.

Shanti: I don't know how to cut down a Christmas tree. When I look at it, I hope it'll just fall down (she walks out)

Scene 2: Christmas tree nursery

Wallah: (to Shanti) **Hey, badmashi! What're you doing in my shop? You weren't thinking of cutting that tree down, were you?**

Shanti: What if it just falls down?

Wallah: Ha! It if falls down, you can have it. (it falls down).

Shanti: I'll take it.

Scene 3: Outdoors by Raj's house

Shanti: (carrying Christmas tree, to Bara Bandar) **Here's your tree. Where do you want me to put it? By your carrom table or your swimming pool?** (they go inside)

Wallah: (at door, to Raj) **Hey, you goonda. You got a sister? She stole a Christmas tree from our yard.**

Shanti: (comes to door) **I didn't steal it. He said if it fell over, I could have it. When I looked at it, it fell over.** (she goes back inside, shouts out) **It was a Christmas miracle!** (comes back outside) **Why are you standing on our veranda? Go home.**

Wallah: I want our tree back!

Shanti: **You said if it fell over, I could have it. Now get off our veranda, or I'll call Bara Bandar!**

Bara (coming to door): **Don't call Bara Bandar. He's decorating the tree.** (wallah sees Bara)

Wallah (cry of alarm): **AAAAAAAAA** (leaves)

Shanti: (to Raj) **Bhaia, do you think I should give that tree back to the wallah?**

Raj: **Why? Are you starting to feel guilty?**

Shanti: **No! He said I could have it if it fell over.**

Raj: **Santa Claus is coming to town.**

Shanti: **Now I feel guilty.**

Scene 4: Christmas tree nursery

Shanti: (with Bara, at door, knocks, wallah opens) **We brought your tree back.**

Wallah: No, keep it. I was wrong. It's yours. I said if it fell over, to keep it.

Shanti: Really? Thank you! Merry Christmas! (they start to walk away)

Bara: (to audience) **Now I have to decorate it all over again.**

Scene 5: Raj's house

Shanti: (to Raj) **I'm practicing drawing Christmas stars.**

Raj: They look more like jalebis to me. (he walks off)

Shanti: (calling after him) **Dunk a Christmas star in your dudh, and you're in trouble!**

Raj: (enters, carrying star) **I'm going to sell Christmas stars door to door.**

Shanti: Trying to make bara paisa, na? Going after those big holiday lakhs, na? (he exits, she pauses, watching, shouts) **Need any help?**

Scene 6: Rajasthan desert

Brother Bandar: (enters, dances with cactus)
    I'm the Bara Bandar's brother. I live out in Rajasthan.
    I'm a simple vegetarian, drink no liquor, chew no paan.

Every year when Christmas comes around, I decorate with smiles,
String the lights upon a cactus, run extension cords for miles,
Then I paint the rocks and bushes, on the wind the baubles fly.
But I hang the stars forever in the wide and cloudless sky.

Scene 7: Door to door, outside Anita's door

Raj: (at door, knocks, Anita answers) **Would you like to buy a Christmas star?**

Anita: What will I do with it after Christmas?

Raj: Would you like to buy a New Year star?

Anita: Know what you're doing? Adding to the over-commercializing of Christmas.

Raj: Not 'til I sell one.

Anita: (grabs it). **Thank you. I love samples.** (slams door).

Raj: I give up! I can't imagine anyone else having as much trouble as I do selling Christmas decorations.
(Bandar walks by with armload of Christmas decorations.)

Lalita: (skates on) **We have a Christmas show at our skating club this year. I could be in it if I had someone to skate with me. I need a handsome, graceful partner.**

Bara: Did you call?

Lalita: No! (he leaves, Manoj enters) **Manoj, please be my partner in the Christmas skating show.**

Manoj: Forget it. We skiers wouldn't be seen in those tippy-toe skates.

Bara: (re-enters) **Looking for a partner?**

Lalita: If you wake up at five AM.

Bara: No!

Lalita: To skate in the Christmas show, we have to practice and practice and practice!

Bara: While the stars are still out?

Lalita: Stop complaining! Getting up early in the morning is good for you.

Bara: I hope so. It's killing me (they leave)

Scene 8: Raj's House

Raj: (to Shanti) **Grandma says when she was a little girl she used to hang up her stocking on Christmas eve. Then, when Christmas morning came, she'd run downstairs and find it filled with apples and oranges!**

Shanti: (looks at her socks) **I can see it now. Three grapes** (she thinks) **I got it!** (exits, off-stage, whooshing sound, sliding sound, scream, crash. Raj reacts)

Raj: What was that?

Shanti: (re-enters, carrying armload of socks, tosses them down) **Match that, Santa!** (Priya and Bandar enter, covered with bits of tree branches, ornaments) **What are you doing?**

Laxman: They're collecting Christmas ornaments. Christmas is decorated in new ways every year.

Shanti: (to Priya and Bara) **You'd look better with a little angel or star on top.**

Act 3   Cards

<u>Scene 1: Raj's house</u>

Shanti: (to Raj) **Hey, bhaia. Are you awake?**

Raj: I am now.

Shanti: I need one hundred rupees.

Raj: One hundred rupees? For what?

Shanti: Stamps. For my Christmas cards.

Raj: Where would I get one hundred rupees?

Shanti: I'll come back when you're not so grumpy.

<u>Scene 2: Outside school</u>

Laxman (to Mamtha): **I'm making my Christmas card list. Could I have your home address?**

Mamtha: Aren't you kind of old for me?

Laxman: I'm not asking you to marry me! I just want to send you a card.

Mamtha: Why do you want to send me a card?

Laxman: I send cards to lots of people.

Mamtha: I thought maybe it was because you like me.

Laxman: Of course, I like you.

Mamtha: Aren't you kind of old for me?

Laxman: I ALREADY TOLD YOU... (sighs) **'Tis the season to be jolly.**

Mamtha: All right, I'll give you my address so you can send me a Christmas card, but this doesn't mean you can come to our house.

Laxman: ALL I'M GOING TO DO IS SEND YOU A CHRISTMAS CARD!

Mamtha: This is my address. You can send my Christmas card there.

Laxman: What about your name?

Mamtha: Today I'm Mamtha. Last week I called myself Joan of Arc, but I also like Jhansi ke Rani.

Laxman: I'll just put down 'her.' (he writes rapidly, puts card in envelop, seals envelope, drops it in mailbox). See? I'm mailing all my Christmas cards.

Mamtha: Is the one you're sending me in there, too?

Laxman: Right in the old mailbox.

Mamtha: Wow.

Scene 3: Outside Raj's house

Shanti: (to Bara) If I'm going to send you a Christmas card, I need to know your address.

Bara: I live here.

Shanti: I'll put down, 'He lives there.' (she walks off)

Bara: No, *here.* (she walks indoors)

Shanti: (to Raj) I'm making my Christmas list. How do you spell your name?

Raj: I'm your bhaia, my name is simply Raj, and you don't even know how to spell my name?

Shanti: I'll put down Ramakrishnan Mohammed Gautam Guru Nanak Mahavir and ask Mom how to spell it. Look at all the people I have to send Christmas cards to.

Raj: If it bothers you, why do you do it?

Shanti: Because if I don't, they'll hate me. Look at Leela. If I don't send her a card, she'll hate me.

Raj: No, she won't.

Shanti: She won't? (crossing off the name). **Goodbye, Leela!** (to Raj) **I keep records of all the people who didn't send me a Christmas card, and then I hold a grudge against them. You look puzzled. Wait 'til you see my list of people who didn't give me any presents.** (she musses around her papers) **Did I send Abha a Christmas card last year?**

Raj: Yes, I think you did.

Shanti: Did she send me one?

Raj: Yes, I think she did.

Shanti: Then I suppose I should send her one.

Raj: Yes, I suppose so.

Shanti: (holding pen in air): **Abha, you are SO lucky!** (to Raj) **Did I send a Christmas card to Mariamman last year?**

Raj: Yes, I remember because you said she didn't send you one.

Shanti: (pauses, thinks) **I think I'll send her one anyway.** (starts to write) **Maybe it'll make her feel bad.** (Raj rolls his eyes. He tries to write, reads aloud).

Raj: Dear Grandma, How have you been? I hope you have a very merry—Oh no, I made a mess.

Shanti: Wish her a merry mess from me, too. It's a good idea to do our Christmas smudging early (door bell rings).

Raj: I'll get it. (Laxman walks in). Help me, Laxman. I want to make special Christmas card for the beautiful Punjabi girl.

Laxman: Draw a tree with some tiny red hearts hanging on it. Then write something personal at the bottom.

Shanti: What's going on? Is my gur-ka-dabba helping my bhaia draw a Christmas card?

Laxman: I'M NOT YOUR GUR-KA-DABBA! (she exits hurriedly) That is so gigantically stupid!

Raj: There! How does that look? I drew a tree with little hearts on it.

Laxman: (reading) Merry Christmas to my gur-ka-dabba?

Raj: (covering his face with shame) It's a family expression.

Laxman: See you, Raj. (he leaves, goes outside to Bara. Raj has face on table. Shanti re-enters)

Shanti: I'm scratching Preeti off my Christmas card list. She didn't send me a card last year, so why should I send her a card this year?

Raj: You don't know anyone named Preeti.

Shanti: That's no excuse (Raj rolls his eyes). I'm trimming my Christmas card list. Goodbye, Saraswati. Tata, Ganesh. Too bad, Ram. (to Raj) Scratched off my Christmas card list. Get lost, Durga. That's the way it goes, Shiva. Bye-bye, Visnu. Forget you, Brahma. (to Raj) I've never had so much fun before in all my life! (Raj rolls his eyes) I've crossed a LOT of names off. I'm down to

one last name...AND THERE GOES GAUTAM! (scratching it deeply, darkly). (to Raj) **Once they get scratched off my list, they never get back! Have you ever been scratched off a Christmas list?**

Raj: I'm not sure.

Shanti: If you ever are, that's what it will look like (holds up paper). **Is it proper to send your teacher a Christmas card?**

Raj: Sure. Why not?

Shanti: Where do I send it?

Raj: To her home.

Shanti: Teachers have homes?

Raj: How'd you like to take part in a cooperative project? I thought maybe we could have some Christmas cards printed this year with both of our names on them. Would you like that?

Shanti: 'Tis the season to be cooperative.

Raj: Just sign your name right here below mine (writes small, speaks softly) **Raj.** (hands over paper).

Shanti: (writes large, speaks loudly) **SHANTI!** (walks out).

Raj: (calling after her) **May the runners of Santa's sleigh slide painfully over your toes!** (he goes offstage)

Laxman: (outside) **I'll read your list and you tell me what you want to do. Do you want to send a Christmas card to Abha?**

Bara: No, let's forget Abha. I don't think she really likes me.

Laxman: How about the Mehtas?

Bara: I don't know. It's hard to decide.

Laxman: How about Shanti?

Bara: She likes me, but I don't know...

Laxman: How about Priya?

Bara: Well, maybe.

Laxman: I know you don't want to send a card to Lalita.

Bara: I'm glad you know that.

Laxman: Saraswati? Durga? Parvati?

Bara: Nope, nope and nope.

Laxman: How about Anita? I think Anita should get a card.

Bara: Maybe you're right.

Laxman: OK, it's settled. You'll send a card to Anita. I'll mail it out today.

Bara: Thank you. (Laxman walks out.) **That's the trouble with having only one stamp. I'll hand-deliver the rest** (walks over to Raj's house, knocks on door, Raj comes to door, Bara hands over card and walks away).

Raj: (reading) **To my owner, Merry Christmas.** (to audience) **It would be nice to have a monkey who remembered my name.**

Scene 4: Lalita's house

Lalita: (to Laxman) **Here, one of your Christmas cards came back. It says, 'No such address.'**

Laxman: It's that girl at school. She's going to drive me crazy!

Lalita: Why do you bother with her?

Laxman: She fascinates me!

Scene 5: Outside Raj's house

Raj: Guess what? You got a Christmas card from Lalita.

Bara: Oh, no!

Raj: You didn't send her one, did you?

Bara: Of course not! I wouldn't send Lalita a rock.

Raj: She wrote a little note on the back of the card.

Bara: I don't want to hear it.

Raj: 'Dear Bara, I hope you have a nice Christmas. I think I'll visit you soon. I'll stop by. Say hi to Raj.'

Bara: If she comes a thousand miles from me, I'll scream!

Raj: It'll be nice to see her again.

Bara: Seeing her again would be like getting malaria twice.

Raj: You've never forgiven her, have you?

Bara: You don't forgive someone who did what she did to me.

Raj: Anyway, here's the card. (he walks indoors)

Bara: She probably doesn't even remember what happened. That would be just like her. She'll come to see me, too. Just what I need—a Lalita Christmas.

Shanti: (to Raj) **I mailed all my Christmas cards.**

Raj: I thought you didn't have any stamps.

Shanti: I drew my own. I drew Babur, Humayun, Akbar, Jehangir, Shah Jahan and Aurangzeb.

Raj: That's illegal.

Bara: (enters house, with briefcase and hat) **Anyone need an advocate?**

Shanti: Do you think I'll get arrested for drawing my own stamps?

Raj: You might start looking for a good wakil.

Bara: Before we begin, your honor, may I ask if you received the Christmas card we sent you?

Scene 6: School

Laxman: (to Mamtha) **May I ask you a simple question.**

Mamtha: Today my name is Cleopatra.

Laxman: OK, Cleopatra, please tell me how I can send you a Christmas card if you give me the wrong address.

Mamtha: Last year we had all blue lights on our tree.

Priya: Hey, Raj. I'm making my Christmas card list and wanted to know your address so I could surprise you with a card. But now the surprise is gone, na? I'll just send your card to someone else so I guess I won't need your address. Forget it, Raj. (Raj sighs) (to Mamtha) **Hey,**

Mamtha. You got any extra Christmas cards? I forgot to buy some. And how about stamps? I'll need some, too. Here, keep this one (hands card over). Then I won't have to send it to you.

Mamtha: It's good to see you so filled with the Christmas spirit.

Priya: 'Tis the season to be sarcastic.

Scene 7: Outside Raj's house

Raj: It's silly for me to wait near the mailbox waiting for Christmas cards. Most people wouldn't check every five minutes. They'd think it's stupid (he walks away).

Bara: (pokes his head around corner) Not at all. If you sit IN the mailbox long enough, you'll get a Christmas card.

Raj: (re-enters, Bara pokes his head out of sight) There's where that beautiful Punjabi girl lives. Maybe she'll see me and rush out to thank me for the Christmas card I sent her. Maybe she'll even hug me. (he pauses). And maybe Sonia Gandhi will also call me tonight and ask me out to dinner.

Scene 8: Lalitha's house

Lalita: (to Laxman) This is for you.

Laxman: Oh, no! It's a Christmas card from Mamtha.

Lalita: You didn't send her one, did you?

Laxman: I couldn't! She wouldn't ever tell me her real address. I've been out-Christmassed!

Scene 9: Door to door, outside Anita's house

Raj: (with Bara, at door, to Anita): **Ask your mom if she'd like to buy some homemade Christmas cards.**

Anita: These are kind of cute.

Raj: Thank you.

Bara: I drew all the bananas.

Anita: But is it appropriate to call someone 'sweetheart' on a Christmas card?

Bara: It is if you can't remember her name.

Scene 10: Raj's house

Shanti: All my Christmas cards came back.

Raj: That's because you drew your own stamps.

Shanti: I copied them from the Great Moghuls.

Bara: (in attorney hat and briefcase) **She drew a better Jehangir than Moghul artists did.**

Shanti: How many Christmas cards did you sell?

Raj: None.

Shanti: How will you buy presents for all your girlfriends?

Raj: I don't have any. I only have a monkey.

Bara: (holding plastic bag) **Any bananas for the monkey?**

Act 4   Gifts

<u>Scene 1: Raj's house</u>

Shanti: (to Raj) **Don't give me anything for Christmas this year, bhaia. All I want is for everyone to have peace, joy and love.**

Raj: Do you really mean that? Are you really sincere?

Shanti: No, I've finally flipped. (to Bara) **If you're making a Christmas list, you can scratch me. I don't want any presents this year.** (he scratches furiously). **Scratching is one thing.** *Obliterating* **is another.** (to Laxman) **I don't want you to give me anything for Christmas this year, either.**

Laxman: Really? That's too bad, but I can understand how you feel and I admire you for it. (shouts offstage) **CANCEL THAT ORDER FOR THE TEN THOUSAND DOLLAR NECKLACE!**

Shanti: After the holidays are over and everything has quieted down, I'm going to beat you. (he leaves hurriedly; she speaks to Raj and Bara) **Everyone should be like me. I've asked for nothing for Christmas. I am totally unselfish. If everyone were like me, this would be a better world** (Bara and Laxman both roll their eyes). **Maybe someone will start a new movement where everyone will try to be like me! I could be the head me!** (Bara sticks his finger down his throat).

<u>Scene 2: Lalitha's House</u>

Lalita: (to Manoj, who is playing the piano) **Christmas will be here soon. Merry Christmas!**

Manoj: Thank you.

Lalita: I've just noticed something about this room.

Manoj: What's that?

Lalita: **There's an appalling lack of mistletoe.** (no response) **I made a list of things you might want to give me.** (she hands it to him; he throws it over his shoulder). **He didn't miss a note. I know why you don't want to buy me anything for Christmas this year. You hate me.**

Manoj: **I never said I hated you.**

Lalita: **THEN BUY ME SOMETHING! Did Ravi Shankar every buy his girlfriend fuzzy gloves for Christmas**

Manoj: **I doubt it.**

Lalita: **Then here's a chance to do something he never did.**

Manoj: **I've already thought of doing something he never did.** (he grabs his instrument, against which she's been leaning, and she falls over. He leaves. Laxman enters)

Laxman: (to Lalita) **You hit me yesterday, remember? Therefore, I've decided not to get you anything for Christmas this year.** (she places her fist against his face) **What are you doing?** (she pulls her fist back quickly)

Lalita: **Taking back a hit. You HAVE to give me a Christmas present. It says so in the Bible.**

Laxman: **You're bluffing. The Bible says nothing about giving Christmas presents.**

Lalita: **It doesn't?**

Laxman: **You can't bluff an old theologian.**

Lalita: (dejected, sighs. suddenly energetic again) **You have to give me a Christmas present. That's the Christmas rule. You can't ignore the Christmas rule!**

Laxman: **I can do anything I want. You hit me so I've decided not to give you a Christmas present** (he walks off).

Lalita: I may have to suffer martyrdom. (idea, she rummages in a book). **Here it is! I found it. I found the word sister in the Bible! There it is! Right there! See?**

Laxman: (walks back on, looks at the book) **So?**

Lalita: There's the word 'sister' right there in the Bible. That PROVES you have to give me a Christmas present. (he rolls his eyes) **Then get out of this house! And take your stupid jacket with you!** (she throws it over his head)

Laxman: You can't throw me out of my own house. I live here, too, you know. You'll never get away with this. Do you hear me!** (he walks off) **She drives me crazy! I'm so mad I feel I'm going to explode!** (he stops) **I don't have to stand for this! I don't have to take this from her** (he walks back) **I 'm going to tell her off like she's never been told off before** (SLAMS door, stalks up to her, glaring).

Lalita: Well?

Laxman: (intensely, teeth barred, gritted) **I hope you don't get *anything* you want for Christmas!**

Scene 3: Raj's house

Shanti: I CAN'T GO THROUGH WITH IT! I have to get Christmas presents. I want all I can get and I want it now before it's too late. I want all I can get before I'm too old and everything is gone and the sun has dimmed and the stars have fallen and the birds are silent and the wheat is eaten.

Raj: The wheat is eaten?

Shanti: So you know what you can give me for Christmas, bhaia? A horse!

Raj: A horse? I don't think I can buy you a horse, but I can buy you a pencil that you can use to underline the listing in the TV guide for the next cowboy movie.

Shanti: Just what I need, a brother with a warped sense of humor.

Raj: 'Tis the season to be jolly.

Shanti: I had to write a Christmas theme for school. Here it is. (reading). 'The True Meaning of Christmas.' To me, Christmas is the joy of getting.

Raj: You mean giving. Christmas is the joy of giving.

Shanti: (to Raj) I don't have the slightest idea what you're talking about. (continues reading) Christmas is getting all you can while the getting is good!

Raj: Giving! The only real joy is giving!

Shanti: (looks at him, pauses, then rolls her eyes) Like, wow. (she starts folding up the paper into a paper airplane). This year I'm going to make all my Christmas presents, and guess what I'm giving everyone? Paper airplanes! (she throws it at him) You're lucky. You got yours early. How many shopping days until Christmas?

Raj: About ten.

Shanti: What did you tell me that for?

Raj: You just asked me!

Shanti: I didn't really want to know. Why should I do any Christmas shopping? I'm not interested in giving, only in getting. Get, get, get! I have a get list!

Raj: Where's your give list?

Shanti: My what?

Raj: I knew it. Well, I tried to earn some money for Christmas. I asked people to give me some work. They asked what I do. I shovel sidewalks, rake leaves and garble messages. No one would hire me. That means I can't buy any Christmas presents this year (he goes outside)

Shanti: (calling after him) If you sold the rake, you could at least buy me something.

Raj: (outside, to Bara) A gift arrived for you.

Bara: (reading) A Christmas present from Nepal! From the Yeti! This is exciting! I wonder what it is. (he opens it). Shoes? What will I do with shoes? I have four hands! Why give somebody something they can't use? (pauses, thinks) I know! I'll send him a swimming suit!

Raj: (back on) Look what I got you for Christmas! A bowl full of chocolate chip cookies!

Bara: Wow!

Raj: (leaving) I just hope you don't eat them all at once.

Bara: (gulps them down, looks up from empty bowl) What did he say? (stares at back door)

Raj: (back on) And you can stop staring at the back door. All the Christmas cookies are gone. I didn't want you to waste a good stare (he leaves)

Bara: How thoughtful! Happiness is a thoughtful friend.

Raj: (back on). I don't know what to get you for Christmas. You're a hard one to shop for (he leaves).

Bara: Not really. I can always use more software for my computer.

Lalita: (coming on) Surprise! Go ahead, open it. I got you this present (he opens it). It's a pair of shoes! You're a hard one to get a present for, but I wanted to get you

something different that a lot of others hadn't already given you. (she leaves. Bara holds up both pairs of shoes, sighs)

Raj: (comes on) **Hi, a package came for you. Oh, you got some presents already?** (Bara holds up two pairs of shoes). **Two pairs of shoes? And you haven't any feet?** (laughs, Bara looks grieved.) **Too bad you don't have a sense of humor. Anyway, this one says, 'Do not open until Christmas'** (leaves)

Bara: **I can't read! Ha ha ha.** (tears open package). **Oh, no, another pair of shoes! He was right. I should have waited. Now everyone else will open presents and I'll just stand around and watch. I'm so stupid. I do this every year.**

Raj: (comes on). **Surprise! Another package came, but it says, 'Do not open until...'**

Bara: (grabs it) **Who cares? I can't wait! I can't wait!** (tears it open). **Oh, no, another pair of shoes! I'm so stupid. Hey, Laxman? Christmas is coming. Have you thought yet about what you're going to get me? Maybe some fruit? Candy?**

Laxman: (coming on). **Here it is. Merry Christmas.**

Bara: **Ah ha!** (tears it open) **Another pair of shoes!**

Lalita: (enters with Raj) **Christmas is coming. I've made out a list to help you decide what to get me.**

Raj: **My hands are full right now. Could you put it some place where I'll remember it** (she attaches it to Raj's tail, she leaves)

Raj: **I saved some Christmas cookies for your friend the neighbor's cat. That was a good idea, na? That will make her happy. I'm glad you agree.**

Bara: (to audience) **Sure, I agree. I ate it.**

Lalita: (enters) **Raj? I made up a new list of things I want for Christmas.**

Raj: I had to admit it, but I can't ever remember where we put the other list.

Lalita: Don't worry. I know just where it is. (spindles the new list on Bara's tail). **I just checked the calendar today. I couldn't believe it. Only a few more shopping days until Christmas.**

Bara: Not if you don't buy anything. (Laxman enters)

Lalita: (to Laxman) **How would you like to see a list of things I want for Christmas?**

Laxman: Absolutely not. I want my gift to you to be a complete and delightful surprise.

Lalita: (starting to cry). **What a lovely, generous thought** (she exits)

Laxman: Off the hook. (exits opposite)

Bara: (to audience). **I read a story. One lady and her husband decided to attend a performance of King Lear. It was their first night out together in months. During the second act, one of the performers became very ill. The manager of the theatre walked onto the stage, and asked, 'Is there a doctor in the house?' Her husband stood and shouted, 'I have an honorary degree from Gateway College!' At that moment, she decided not to get him anything for Christmas.**

Scene 4: Shop

Raj: (enters with Shanti, Bara, and Lalita) **There are too many things these days to worry about.**

Laxman: I agree.

Raj: (to wallah) **I'd like to buy a Christmas present for a pretty Punjabi girl I know. I was thinking maybe a pair of gloves. Would it help if I described her? She has ten fingers.**

Wallah: One hundred rupees.

Raj: One hundred rupees?!

Shanti: She'll be disappointed when she finds out her boyfriend is a cheapskate.

Raj: I'm not a cheapskate. I just don't have one hundred rupees.

Shanti: Put it on your credit card.

Raj: I don't have a credit card.

Shanti: Too bad, Punjabi girl!

Raj: (to Laxman) **I'd like to give her a nice pair of gloves for Christmas, but I can't afford it.**

Laxman: If she really likes you, Raj, she'll appreciate anything you give her.

Lalita: If you don't give her exactly what she's expecting, she'll hate you for the rest of your life.

Bara: Fortunately, I don't have to be involved.

Laxman: Why do you want to buy her those gloves for Christmas?

Raj: When I first met her last summer, I noticed what pretty hands she had. I want those pretty hands to be warm. But I don't have one hundred rupees for the gloves.

Laxman: Send her a nice card and tell her to keep her hands in her pockets.

Raj: (to Lalita) **See? Those gloves I'd like to buy the pretty Punjabi girl for Christmas.**

Lalita: Where will you get the one hundred rupees?

Raj: That's the problem.

Lalita: Maybe you could sell your monkey. (looks at Bara, who sticks out his tongue at her). **I take that back. He's probably worth only fifty paisa.**

Shanti: But selling the monkey is a great idea! (Bara kicks her in the shins) **Ow!** (he exits, running, Shanti limping after him, Lalita following)

Raj: Sahib. I need your advice. Do you think I should spend my last ten rupees on a Christmas present for a girl who doesn't know I even exist? Thank you. (to Laxman as they walk out). **I just saved ten rupees.**

Act 5   Santa

Raj: And then, on Christmas evening, Santa Claus comes down the chimney. He leaves the toys on the hearth, goes back up the chimney and flies off through the air in his sled. (pause). Somehow, I sense an element of doubt.

Lalita: You mean Santa Claus comes down this chimney, then crawls out this fireplace, and he does that in every house in town?

Raj: All over the world!

Lalita: What a way to make a living! (to Laxman) He stops at every house in the whole world, climbs down every chimney and leaves a present for every boy and every girl, all in one night.

Laxman: Wow. That's hard to believe. That's awfully hard to believe...BUT I BELIEVE IT! He must be highly skilled.

Manoj: What's he really like? It's just not natural for someone to go around giving away all those presents.

Raj: You know I think? He does it because he feels guilty about something!

Lalita: What if Santa Claus gets picked up on a radar screen someplace and what if they shoot him down with a guided missile? What then, Raj?

Raj: That's the way it goes.

Lalita: That's no consolation!

Raj: Santa Claus gets letters from millions of kids all over the world.

Lalita: Amazing!

Raj: And he reads all those letters one by one to see what the kids want.

Lalita: Incredible.

Raj: Then on Christmas Eve he delivers all those things right to their doors!

Lalita: What a marvelous age we live in!

Scene 2: School

Shanti: (to audience and cast) **This is my Christmas story, 'Santa and His Rain Gear'. When Santa left the North Pole that evening, a gentle mist was falling. In his yellow slicker and big rubber boots, he set out on his annual journey. It was Christmas eve, and soon children all over the world would be hearing the sound of Santa and his rain gear. Little George was waiting for Santa to come. Suddenly, he heard the sound of someone walking on the roof! It was a man in a yellow slicker and big rubber boots. 'I saw him' shouted little George. 'I saw Santa and his rain gear.' Don't squirm. There's more to come. 'The rain came down harder and harder, but the man in the yellow slicker and big rubber boots never faltered. Another Christmas Eve had passed, and Santa and his rain gear had done their job. The end.**

All cast: **HA HA HA HA** (laughing loudly)

Scene 3: Raj's house

Shanti: **Everyone laughed at my story. Ha! How about this thing with all the reindeer pulling a sleigh through the air? No way. I don't care how many reindeer he had, they** could never produce enough lift to get a sled in the air. No way, na, bhaia?

Raj: No way. Merry Christmas.

Anita: Is this your letter, Raj, to Santa Claus?

Raj: Yeah.

Anita: It sounds a lot like the one you wrote last Christmas.

Raj: It is. This form letter goes out every year.

Lalita: Mr. Claus c/o North Pole. Dear Joe,

Laxman: Joe?

Lalita: He hates to be called Santa.

Shanti: Dear Joe Claus,

Lalita: (looks at watch) We have to go. C'mon, Laxman.

Laxman: See you soon.

Raj: Bye. (they leave. To Shanti) His name is Santa, not Joe.

Shanti: (crumbles up old paper) I didn't think that looked right. Where's a good pen? I need some extra nice stationery. (writes) Dear Samantha Claus.

Raj: Samantha Claus?

Shanti: She's the fat lady with the reindeer who brings us Christmas presents.

Raj: With the red suit and the white beard?

Shanti: The white beard is just a sort of disguise.

Raj: Very clever.

Shanti: Shall I ask her to bring you a new bicycle?

Raj: Why not?

Shanti: (writing) **Please bring my brother a bicycle.**

Raj: Does Samantha Claus go, 'Ho ho ho' or does she just smile daintily?

Shanti: (writing) **Forget the bicycle** (he rolls his eyes)

Scene 4 Raj's house

Shanti: I should have known!

Raj: Should have known what?

Shanti: Why didn't you tell me?

Raj: Tell you what?

Shanti: That there is no Samantha Claus. The kids at school all laughed at me. Why didn't you TELL me? Samantha Claus. Santa Claus. They sound alike. How was I to know? They all laughed at me. I made a complete fool or myself. I'm ruined for life. I have nothing to live for. You're not listening to me. What are you doing with that stupid box?

Raj: Wrapping your Christmas present.

Shanti: This has always been my favorite time of year. (she gets out paper) **Dear Santa Claus.** (to Raj) **Any middle initial?**

Raj: No, I don't think so. AT least I've never heard of one.

Shanti: Does he have a title or a rank?

Raj: I don't know. I never thought about it.

Shanti: I'll put down lieutenant colonel. (writes) **I saw a recent picture of you in a magazine. You look fatter than ever. I know how you usually fly through the air with your reindeer and sleigh. I'll be surprised this year if you even get off the ground.** (knock on door)

Raj: I'll get it (Lalita and Laxman walk in)

Lalita: We came to finish our Christmas letters with you. (sits down, starts writing) **Dear Santa Claus, Just a note before you take off. I always worry about you. I hope you are in good health. Please drive carefully. Have a good trip. Affectionately yours. Lalita Sharma, your friend. P.S. Merry Christmas. Lalita, your very good friend.** (she kisses the letter several times, Laxman goes bleah, gets out his own paper).

Laxman: Dear Santa Claus, how are all your reindeer? Are they well fed? Is your sleigh in good shape? Are the runners oiled? Then go, man, GO! (he crumbles up that page) I don't think I'd better send that.

Shanti: Dear Monsieur Claus,

Raj: Monsieur Claus?

Shanti: I suppose it never occurred to you that he might be French? I thought it might be nice also to drop a little note to Santa Claus' wife. (writes) **Dear Signora Claus**

Raj: Signora?

Shanti: I have a theory he married a nice Italian girl. Do you know his wife's name?

Raj: Well, sometimes people say her name is Mary Christmas.

Shanti: Really? That's very interesting. Maybe I'll write her instead. (sits, writes) **Dear Mary Christmas, Congratulations on deciding to keep your own name.** (new page, writes) **Dear Santa Claus, Do you need a secretary to help during the holiday season? I could answer letters and run errands, and I will work for only five thousand rupees per week.**

Raj: Five thousand rupees per week?

Shanti: Why not? Everyone knows the old guy is loaded. (he rolls his eyes)

Raj: Hey, everybody, Santa Claus answered one of my letters.

Anita: Open it, let's see what he wrote!

Raj: Oh, no.

Anita: What is it?

Raj: A circular rejection slip. So I'd better write a personal letter (gets out paper)

Lalita: Dear Santa, Gimme a bicycle, gimme a puppy, gimme a doll, gimme a camera, gimme a doll buggy and gimme some candy. Yours truly, Lalita. Gimme, gimme, gimme, gimme, gimme!

Shanti: Dear Snooty Claus,

Raj: Snooty Claus?

Shanti: He thinks he's so smart. He didn't bring me anything I wanted last year.

Raj: Well, don't burn your bridges.

Shanti: What do bridges have to do with it? (he goes back to his writing) **Now I forgot what I was writing.**

Laxman: Dear Santa Claus, How have you been? Please don't get the idea that I am writing because I want something. Nothing could be farther from the truth. I want nothing. If you want to skip our house this year, go right ahead. I won't be offended. Really I won't. Spend your time elsewhere. Don't bother with me. I really mean it.

Lalita: WHAT IN THE WORLD KIND OF LETTER IS THIS?

Laxman: I hope he'll find my attitude peculiarly refreshing.

Lalita: (grabs it, crumbles it up). **We're not taking any chance at our house, we're not. Write another one.**

Laxman: Dear Santa Claus, How have you been? How is your wife? I am not sure what I want for Christmas this year. Sometimes it is very hard to decide. Perhaps you should send me your catalogue.

Raj: Dear Santa Claus, I don't want any toys this year. I would much rather have a photograph or yourself to hang on the wall of my room (smiles, to audience) **Psychology.**

Laxman: Dear Santa Claus, Enclosed please find a list of things I want for Christmas. Also, please note indication of size, color and quantity of each item listed.

Raj: Wow, how efficient can you get?

Laxman: I'm going now. See you when we visit Santa at the mall. (he and Lalita exit)

Raj: (to Anita) **I wrote a new letter to Santa Claus** (hands it over)

Anita: (reading, starts to sniff, sob) **Boo hoo hoo, waaaa** (breaks down crying, exits)

Raj: Pretty heart-rending, isn't it?

Shanti: Dear Santa Claus,

Raj: (to audience) **Actually, there is no Santa Claus**

Shanti: **This year, please bring me a camera, a pony and a bicycle.**

Raj: (to audience) **There comes a time when we have to stop trusting legends.**

Shanti: **some money, a desk, a goldfish, a MP3 player, a bracelet...**

Raj: (to audience) **As we grow older, we have to face life's realities...**

Shanti: **a hair dryer, a radio, a portable TV and some sweaters and dresses.**

Raj: (to audience) **Myths have to be replaced by truth.**

Shanti: (to Raj) **Do you want me to put you down for a baseball glove?**

Raj: **Yes, that would be very nice.**

Shanti: (writing) **...and a baseball glove for my brother**

Raj: (to audience) **'Tis the season to be wishy-washy.**

Shanti: **Dear Santa Claus, How have you been** (to Raj) **I feel like an idiot writing to someone who doesn't exist. On the other hand, if he really does exist and I don't write, I'd feel even dumber.**

Raj: **This is the time of year when it's best to touch all the bases.**

Shanti: **Whatever that means** (pauses) **I hear someone on our roof. Do you think it could be Santa and his reindeer?**
Raj: **No, I'm afraid it's just the TV repairman.**

Shanti: That's even better! (door knocks) I'll get it (Manoj enters, bursts in)

Manoj: Hi, Shanti. Raj, I've got this whole Santa Claus bit figured out. If there IS a Santa Claus, he's going to be too nice not to bring me anything for Christmas no matter how I act, right? Right! And if there's ISN'T any Santa Claus, they I haven't lost anything, right? (shrugs, exits)

Raj: Wrong. But I don't know where.

Shanti: Hey, he's right. If you're good, Santa Claus brings you presents, right?

Raj: Right.

Shanti: And if you're not good, he doesn't bring you presents, right?

Raj: Right.

Shanti: Wrong! Have you ever heard of one case where that actually happened? Never! That old rascal is bluffing. I'm writing him a letter.

Shanti: Dear Santa Claus, you can't bluff me. I know that you are wishy-washy. I know that you will bring me presents whether I'm good or whether I'm bad. Shanti (folds up letter) I'm posting this. Into the teeth of the storm (she exits)

Scene 5: mall

Shanti: (to Raj) Look at Santa up there! Talk about fat city. I can't believe he can crawl up and down all those chimneys without losing a little weight. Do you know what's going to happen one of these times? He's going to have a coronary right in some poor little kid's living room.

Raj: Don't worry about it. Merry Christmas.

Shanti: It could be OUR living room. (to kid in front) **Is this the line to see Santa Claus?**

Anita: I hope so.

Shanti: He sure looks fat, doesn't he? Weight loss in patients with a large stomach may improve walking, and thus lead to fewer anginal attacks.

Anita: Maybe I am in the wrong line. (exits)

Laxman: (to Lalita) When I get up there to see Santa, should I ask for a bicycle or a monkey? I think maybe a monkey. You can't fall off a monkey (Lalita exits, he speaks to Bara) When Santa Claus brings me a monkey, I won't have to borrow you anymore from Raj. I'll get a hoop and my new monkey that Santa Claus will bring me will jump through it. Anyway, I want to thank you for all the good times we've had. I'll probably call my new monkey Bhim. Bhim Bandar. I'll say, 'Here, Bhim, jump through the hoop!'

Bara: Look out, Bhim. (thought occurs) When Scrooge was younger, he had a sentimental, sad but inspiring monkey who everyone loved, called Tiny Jim, but the monkey later left him.

Laxman: (to Raj) When Santa Claus brings me the monkey, will he leave it on the front porch or in the back yard? He wouldn't drop it down the chimney, would he?

Raj: There's something I think I should tell you.

Laxman: Maybe he'll just leave a gift certificate. Then I'll go to the store and say, 'Santa Claus is bringing me a monkey, so I need a leash, a collar and a food dish, and you can put it on my tab.'

Raj: They'll throw you out.

Laxman: I guess you're right   Sigh. (to Bara) **Who am
I kidding? Santa Claus will never bring a monkey to
someone whose mom doesn't want him to have a monkey.
If I'm lucky, I'll get a pair of socks and an orange.**

Bara: **If I get a rubber banana, I'll share it.** (Laxman exits)

Shanti: (to Bara) **Did you ever think about Santa Claus
having a coronary?**

Bara: **A what?**

Shanti: **When you get up there to talk to him, check his
ear lobes.**

Bara: **Do what?**

Shanti: **A deep crease in the ear lobes could indicate
change in coronary vessels. Check his ear lobes.**

Bara: **Do what?**

Shanti: (calling offstage) **Mr. Santa Claus? My name is
Shanti. I'm concerned about your weight. When was the
last time you had a stress test? How is your cholesterol?
Do you have a crease in your ear lobes? Just let me check
those ear lobes.**

Santa: (voice offstage) **Hey!**

Shanti: **Don't push me. Just because you're Santa Claus
doesn't mean you can throw me out. Don't push me. I
was trying to help you. You're too fat. AND YOU HAVE A
CREASE IN YOUR EAR LOBE!** (she exits)

Lalita: **Did you tell Santa Claus what you want for
Christmas?**

Laxman: **Sure. I also wished him a happy Hanukkah.
We didn't have much time, but we discussed Judas
Maccabaeus and the cleansing of the temple. You don't
often find a Santa Claus interested in religion.** (to Bara) **As**

far as gifts go, I'm not complaining. I simply learned we shouldn't always expect everything we ask for.

Bara: That's called preaching to the choir.

Scene 6: Raj's house

Shanti: (to Raj) **What's on TV?**

Raj: **Just news. A department store Santa had a heart attack. They took him to the hospital, and he had triple bypass surgery. They said that just before his heart attack, there was some kind of disturbance by a little girl at the store** (they walk out)

Bara: (outside) **I don't think I'll tell my brother there's no Santa. He exchanged gifts with a rock and hung his stocking on a cactus in Rajasthan. He strung a 'Merry Christmas' banner upside down between the rock and the cactus. He'll never get any presents. Nor me. We're the lowest of the low. Old Santa Claus doesn't even know we exist, couldn't care less about nondescript, nobody monkeys. We count for nothing. That old guy won't bring presents. It's kind of sad at Christmastime to be a nobody monkey. Kind of sad to be alone just before every Christmas. Though I've told him Santa has never, in entire recorded history, filled a stray monkey's sock, that doesn't discourage him. He feels the odds are with him. But if he's going to be visited by the old fellow in the red suit, I'll have to do it. It's only right to show compassion this time of year. I'll be the new, improved Santa Claus. Raj and Shanti probably also need cheering up.** (offstage, Raj and Shanti singing carols) **What's that? They're singing carols? Those poor humans are cheering themselves up. They don't need me. Suddenly the loneliness of my days is too much for me to bear. I'll cry out in terrible anguish. AAAAAAAUGH.**

Shanti: (pokes her head outdoors) **What was that?**

Raj: (pokes his head outdoors) **Let's not sing any more Christmas carols. When you're a long way from home, they can be very depressing** (withdraws indoors)

Shanti: (to audience) **Sometimes I have no idea what he's talking about.** (withdraws indoors)

Bara: Not only that, but my bit of jungle has been replaced by a highway. That's sad. (to audience) **Gotta put a politically correct plug in this play.**

Mamtha: (walking by, eating lunch, to Priya) **Look what Mom put in my lunch for us—Christmas cookies!**

Priya: Wow! A whole bunch! Too bad we don't have someone to share them with (Bara grabs the cookies, exits running. The girls, shouting, exit, chasing him).

Scene 7: Mall

Raj: (enters with Bara) **This is embarrassing. Why couldn't you walk here by yourself?** (Bara gets bell and bucket marked 'donations,' starts ringing bell) **Try it without the red nose** (Bara removes red nose) **And here's a little snack for while you work** (Raj exits).

Laxman: (enters with Lalita) **Look, Santa Claus is eating out of a bandar bowl!**

Lalita: Tell Santa what you want for Christmas.

Laxman: I'd like some books, a video game, some in-line skates and maybe a nice sweater.

Lalita: That was great. Now you have something to look forward to on Christmas morning.

Laxman: Before we go any farther, could I ask you something? Did you know I was talking to a bandar?

Lalita: Perhaps it is my didi duty to tell you what you see is not really Santa Claus. You're looking at a bandar in a Santa Claus suit. Now that I've told you this, how do you feel?

Laxman: (hugs Bara) He needs a secretary, but I like the Santa Bandar. I have no money and I feel guilty not giving him anything.

Lalita: (walking away) Don't worry about it. He can't remember everyone who walks by.

Bara: Dark hair, beady eyes, checkered coat.

Shanti: And this year I want a red bicycle, some rollerblades, a blue sweater, and...Are you listening to me?

Bara: I can't hear a thing. Someone around here keeps ringing a bell.

Laxman: Why don't you get rid of that bell so you can hear what I want for Christmas? (Bara throws it away.) So, Mr. Fancy Claus, what happened to all the things you were going to bring me for Christmas last year? Kind of forgot, didn't you? I don't suppose you'd care to explain, would you, huh? (Bara roars at him, Laxman backs away in alarm) He seems pretty busy.

Lalita: (walking back in) If you're really Santa Claus, why aren't you flying around with your reindeer? How will you land on all those rooftops and go down all those chimneys? And after you go down a chimney, how will you get back up? And even if you do, what makes you think your reindeer will be waiting for you. I give you about three houses, and you'll be completely exhausted. (Bara grabs bell, pushes it at her face)

Manoj: Yeah, Santa, get going on your trip.

Shanti: Don't you know it's almost Christmas? (pause) **I don't think you're a real Santa Claus. If you are, where are your helpers?** (two helpers walk by, carrying signs saying, 'Help'). **That's the dumbest thing I've ever seen.**

Bara: Who cares? Merry Christmas! Ook, ook.

Raj: There are too many things today to worry about.

Laxman: I agree. I never thought I'd have to worry about tripping over one of Santa Claus' helpers.

Lalita: I suppose he'll start ringing that bell again and we'll have to listen to it every time we walk by here.

Anita: Don't you think he could do something besides ring a bell? (Bara honks horn)

Lalita: (to Laxman) **Just ignore him, bhai. He can't do anything to you.** (Bara honks horn, Laxman jumps. Bara puts down horn, starts playing harmonium, to Laxman) **To me, 'Kesaria' doesn't sound very Christmassy.**

Raj: Christmas eve is my favorite day of the year. It makes me feel good about everything. I wish I could put it into words.

Bara: My aerobics class was cancelled.

Raj: Sometimes I'm actually afraid to be happy. Every time I'm happy, something bad happens.

Laxman: Nonsense, Raj. Have a very merry Christmas.

Raj: NOW YOU DID IT!

Act 6   Programs

Lalita: All right, who can tell me something about Christmas?

Manoj: The Maharajah of Mysore used to throw big Christmas parties at his house.

Lalita: He did not! Where do you get these ideas?

Manoj: When he was little, the maharajah got a sled for Christmas and he called it 'Jantar Mantar.'

Lalita: I can't stand it! All right, who can tell me why we put a star on top of our Christmas trees?

Manoj: The maharajah used to see a green star on the top of the Nizam of Hyderabad's tree.

Lalita: He did not! You stupid kid!

Anita: You shouldn't yell at someone just before Christmas.

Lalita: Tuition is over! Jao! (they exit with injured expressions on their faces)

Laxman: (enters) **Riding on the back of Mom's bicycle, I'm a white knuckle flier. 'Look out for the tree! Look out for the fence! Jingle Bells—look out! Jingle bells—look out! Jingle all the—look out--way!' Singing doesn't help.**

Lalita: (leaning on keyboard, to Manoj, who plays) **Did Ravi Shankar ever play 'Jingle Bells'? He probably thought he was too good to play Jingle Bells.** (Manoj grabs keyboard away, she falls over, he exits) **If I had met him, I would have said, "Hey, Ravi, old boy, play 'Jingle Bells'."** (to Laxman) **A lady from the panchayat visited. I volunteered you to sing 'Jingle Bells' in the Christmas program.**

49

Laxman: You WHAT? I CAN'T SING. YOU KNOW THAT! I'VE NEVER BEEN ABLE TO SING!

Lalita: Learn. (Raj enters)

Laxman: (slumping in seat) **Raj, Lalita volunteered me to sing 'Jingle Bells' at the panchayat Christmas program. I can't sing in public! I'm a terrible singer. I never have been able to sing.**

Raj: Don't worry about it. In Psalm 98, we read, 'Make a joyful noise to the Lord.'

Laxman: THIS IS THE PANCHAYAT! (to Bara) **Do you know how to destroy a child's holiday season? Make him take part in a Christmas program. Tell him he has to sing 'Jingle Bells' in front of the whole panchayat. THAT'S HOW TO DESTROY A CHILD'S HOLIDAY SEASON** (Bara backs away quickly)

Shanti: (enters) **Guess what? I've been asked to be in a Christmas play. I'm going to be an angel. All I have to do is say, 'Hark'.**

Laxman: I'll trade places.

Lalita: No, you won't! (she grabs him, starts dragging him away).

Laxman: Wish me luck, Raj. I'm on my way to the panchayat Christmas program to sing 'Jingle Bells'.

Raj: Good luck!

Scene 2: Raj's house

Lalita: He thought he could pull a fast one in front of the whole panchayat.

Raj: What did he do?

50

Laxman: (to Lalita) **Thou speakest harsh words at yuletide.** (to Raj) **I said Christmas is to be a time of peace on earth, not a time of ruining a child's holiday season by making him take part in Christmas programs.**

Raj: (to Lalita) **What did you do?**

Lalita: Shouted at him, 'SING, YOU IDIOT.'

Raj: (to Laxman) **What did you do?**

Laxman: (sings) **Jingle bells, jingle bells, jingle all the way.**

Shanti: This is what I have to do in our school Christmas play. When the sheep are through dancing, I come out and say, 'Hark.' Then Harold Angel sings.

Raj: Harold Angel?

Shanti: It's right here in the script. I need to practice my line. 'Hark.' How do I sound? I live in mortal dread of getting out on the stage and forgetting what I'm to say.

Raj: If you did, you could always make up something.

Shanti: That's true. How about 'Hey!'?

Raj: Not very Biblical.

Shanti: Well, that's my line. See if I get it right. 'Hark!'

Raj: You got it. I've always wondered how actors remembered all those lines.

Shanti: Do I look like an angel?

Raj: You look fine. If you had your wings on, you could just fly to the program.

Shanti: (sarcastic) **Ha ha.** (to Laxman) **Hi. I'm writing a Christmas play for our Sunday School. In the opening scene, Nehru talks to Mary.**

Raj: It wasn't Nehru. It was Gabriel.

Shanti: Really? The kid who plays Nehru will be very disappointed. (on phone). **Hello, Manoj, I'm calling about the Christmas play. Apparently I made a little mistake. No, you won't be playing Nehru after all. You'll be someone called Gabriel. Sure, I know how you feel. You can use the coat and rose some other time.** (hangs up, to Laxman) **Now he's upset because he can't be Nehru and come across the stage in a Nehru coat and rose.**

Laxman: Well, maybe he'll get over being upset.

Manoj: (onstage, in Nehru coat with rose) **You said I could be Nehru!**

Shanti: Stop bothering me or I'll change your part to a sheep.

Manoj: BAA

Shanti: BAA to you, too.

Raj: (on phone). **Yes?** (puts phone down). **The Sunday school teacher just canceled your Christmas play.**

Shanti: What?

Raj: It was too controversial.

Shanti: How could it be controversial? I didn't even understand it.

Laxman: Who cancelled it?

Shanti: The Sunday school teacher. I thought I wrote a good play, too. My best scene was where Joseph drives his family to Egypt in a Rolls Royce Silver Shadow.

Manoj: You said I could be—

Shanti: Look, Manoj, don't blame me. Blame the Sunday school teacher.

Manoj: Christmas play—

Shanti: No Christmas play.

Manoj: Nehru—

Shanti: You won't be Nehru or Gabriel or anyone.

Manoj: I memorized all my lines.

Shanti: Forget them. Rub an eraser on your head.

Laxman: I'm sorry your Christmas play was cancelled. They'll probably also say no Christmas tree, Christmas cookies or Christmas carols. (phone rings).

Shanti: (on phone) I see. Thank you. Hey, Manoj, guess what? There's been a compromise. They say we can have a Christmas play as long as it's desi. How would you like to be Nehru? (knock on door).

Manoj: Even better than trekking.

Priya: (enters with Mamtha) I wanted to be Mary in our church play.

Mamtha: The teacher asked me instead.

Priya: Mary never wore glasses. Did she?

Raj: Who?

Priya: Mary in the Bible! Does it say anything about Mary wearing glasses?

Raj: Not really.

Priya: Then how can Mamtha play Mary instead of me, and the teacher says I'm going to play a sheep?

Mamtha: You'll look cute in your sheep costume, Priya.

Priya: Sure, Mamtha, sure.

Mamtha: I was up late last night memorizing all my lines.

Priya: (sarcastic) All your lines.

Mamtha: Excuse me. I must leave. We'll rehearse our first scene.

Priya: BAAA. Who wants to be in a Christmas play if they make you a sheep? A sheep doesn't do anything.

Mamtha: They want you to rehearse your lines.

Priya: BLEAH. Another Christmas play and I have to be a sheep again. I hate being a sheep.

Mamtha: No part in a play is small if it brings joy to the audience.

Priya: Baa.

Mamtha: You do that well.

Lalita: Here's your part for the church Christmas program.

Laxman: Oh, no. Don't tell me! Not again (she hands over paper, he reads) 'So the words spoken through Jeremiah the prophet were fulfilled: a voice was heard in Rama, wailing and loud laments; and it was Rachel weeping for her children, and refusing all consolation because they were no more.

Lalita: Memorize it and be ready to recite it.

Laxman: I can't memorize something like this in a week. This is going to take RESEARCH. Who was Jeremiah? Where was Rama? Why was Rachel so upset? I can't recite something without knowing the who, the where and the why.

Lalita: I'll tell you the who the where and the why. You start memorizing right now or you know who will hit you and where she'll hit you and why she hit you!

Laxman: Christmas isn't only getting too commercial. It's getting too dangerous.

Raj: (to Bara) I'm going to be a shepherd in the Christmas play. This is the piece I have to memorize. 'And there were in the same country shepherds abiding in the fields, keeping watch over their flock by night.'

Shanti: That's a good line. I wonder who wrote it.

Raj: (to Bara) You'll be in the Christmas play, too. You'll be a sheep. Do you think you can imitate a sheep?

Bara: No problem. One monkey is worth a whole flock of sheep any time. (sings) Four calling birds, three French hens...

Shanti: That song drives me crazy. What's a calling bird?

Laxman: A kind of partridge. In 1 Samuel 26.20, it says, 'for the king of Israel has come out to seek my life just as though he were hunting the calling bird. There's a play on words, here, you see. David was standing on a mountain calling and he compared himself to a partridge being hunted. Isn't that fascinating?

Shanti: If I get socks again for Christmas this year, I'll go even crazier.

Laxman: In those days a decree went out from Caesar Augustus. The census is said to have been to 'all the world.' This probably meant only the Roman Empire.

When we read that there was no room at the inn, some scholars feel that the inn more likely was a private home with a guest room. The intention, of course, is to contrast a place of human lodging with a place for feeding animals. When Jesus was born, they laid him in a manger because there was no room for them in the inn. Luke 2.7. Manger could also be confusing here so some scholars think perhaps the—

Shanti: Wouldn't it be neat to have a Christmas tree completely covered with just candy canes?

Laxman: In Luke, the second chapter, the RSV translates as 'Peace among men with whom he is pleased'. This indicates that divine peace is not dependent on human attitudes. The name Bethlehem is interesting, too. It means House of Bread. I think things like this are fascinating. What do you think?

Shanti: I think if I don't get everything I want for Christmas this year, I'm going to gross out. (Laxman rolls his eyes)

Laxman: There were three wise men, see. They came from the east, and they were looking for Bethlehem. You know how they found it? They followed a star.

Shanti: Who was the star?

Laxman: You've heard of Gethsemane, haven't you? This is the Garden of Gethsemane. And this is the Mount of Olives. And this is the Sea of Galilee. And look, here's Bethlehem.

Shanti: That's neat. Where's the Taj Mahal?

Laxman: Taj Mahal?

Shanti: I thought somebody was buried in the Taj Mahal.

Laxman: You don't know anything about Christmas, do you?

Shanti: I know I should get my share of the loot.

Laxman: I can't stand it (Raj enters)

Raj: What's going on here?

Shanti: Look at this picture of Jerusalem. See that dome? Isn't that the Taj Mahal?

Laxman: First you must realize that Luke and Acts were in reality a two-volume work. Note the role of Gabriel. He also appears in Revelations and Daniel. Ask yourself what 'finding favor' really meant to Mary. Check out Hosea 11.1. Read chapter two of First Samuel and the One Hundred and Third Psalm.

Raj: All I ever knew about was the star and the sheep on the hillside.

Laxman: Merry Christmas, Raj.

Scene 3: Raj's house

Shanti: Psst, bhaia, I hate to wake you on Christmas eve, but I need your advice. I was sound asleep when all of a sudden visions of sugarplums danced in my head. What are sugarplums?

Raj: They're sort of round pieces of candy.

Shanti: Good. I was afraid I was freaking out.

Raj: You probably remembered them from the poem.

Shanti: What poem?

Raj: (gets out of bed)
       **'Twas the night before Christmas
           and all through the house,**

> not a creature was stirring,
> not even a mouse.'

Before I continue, here is a brief word from the sponsor. Would you like to buy a magazine?

Shanti: You're trying to sell me a magazine on Christmas eve when I already won't get any presents?

Raj: No presents?

Shanti: Yes. Here is it Christmas eve, but there'll be no sleigh bells outside my window tonight because I've totally rejected the concept of the fat guy in the red suit. For the first time in my life, I feel free. For once I (listens, sits up) **What was that? I thought I heard a sleigh bell. Why can't a person be sure?**

Raj: I just remembered. Aren't we supposed to leave something under the Christmas tree for Santa Claus?

Shanti: How about frozen broccoli? April Fool! I'm leaving a plate of cookies under our tree for Santa Claus, and if I hide someplace, maybe I'll even get to see him. (Bara enters, grabs cookies, exits, running with them). **It worked! I saw him Santa Claus! I never realized he was so hairy!**

Scene 4   Raj's house

Raj: Wake up, Shanti. Get up! Its Christmas morning.

Shanti: I'm afraid. What if I was wrong about this whole stupid Santa Claus thing? What if there aren't any presents for me. I'm afraid to get up and look.

Raj: Santa Claus came last night and didn't leave you anything. (she lies there, dazed) **Just kidding.** (holds up presents) **Merry Christmas!**

Shanti: I WAS RIGHT! Hooray! There is no Santa! Christmas is really about something else!

<u>Scene 5: Lalita's house</u>

Lalita: I stayed up all night last night and I never saw Santa Claus. I'm beginning to suspect something.

Laxman: You don't mean. Surely you don't mean...

Lalita: I do.

Laxman: HORRORS!

Lalita: (pause) Well, why are you standing around? Aren't you going to get ready?

Laxman: I don't know.

Lalita: What do you mean, you don't know?

Laxman: I don't know if I'll be in the Christmas program or not.

Lalita: All right then, DON'T. (door knocks, she opens, Raj enters).

Raj: How do I look?

Laxman: Long pants sure do make the man.

Lalita: (glowers at Laxman, speaks to Raj) Fine. It's the first time I've seen you in a white shirt in six months. Are you sure you know your piece for the Christmas program?

Raj: I know it backwards, forwards, sideways and upside down. I could say it in my sleep.

Lalita: Yeah, well, Laxman says he can't memorize a simple little piece. Why should I care? Remember last year? He almost goofed the whole program.

Raj: Well, this is me and I didn't forget. 'And the angel said unto them, "Fear not. For behold, I bring you good tidings of great joy, which shall be to all people".'

Lalita: Say, that's pretty good.

Raj: I told you I knew it. I have a memory like the proverbial elephant. Well, I'm going on ahead to the church. I'll see you there. (exits, as he walks along outside) 'For behold, I bring you good tidings of great joy, which shall be to all people.' What a memory!

Lalita: (in house still, to Laxman) Why should I always have to worry about you? You'll be the one who gets in trouble, not me. I'll leave without you. That's what I'll do. (she goes out, meets Raj at door). What in the world? I thought you just left.

Raj: I did, but I came back. I forgot where the church is.

Lalita: (she exits, they walk together outside) The street is very slippery with the rain. Brothers are a real nuisance. He could have memorized that piece if he wanted to. (Mamtha and Priya in sheep's costume walk by).

Priya: Every time there's a Christmas play, I end up being a sheep.

Mamtha: Watch out for the curb here.

Priya: What? (falls over).

Mamtha: Slouching toward Bethlehem, na?

Priya: I can't stand it. I wonder if this happens to Laurence Olivier. I can't remember my lines.

Mamtha: You're a sheep. All you have to do is say, BAA.

Priya: I'll never remember it. Why do they have to spoil Christmas by making us be in plays?

Lalita: You sound like Laxman. I don't care if Laxman stays home. What do I care about him?

Laxman: (comes running by, slides, to Lalita) 'So the words spoken through Jeremiah the prophet were fulfilled. "A voice was heard in Rama, wailing and loud laments. It was Rachel weeping for her children, and refusing all consolation, because they were no more".' Matthew 2.17 (he runs onward, exits)

Lalita: (shouting after him) Merry Christmas, bhai!

Laxman: (offstage) Merry Christmas, didi!

Scene 6: Stage at performance

Manoj: (in Nehru coat) I am Ne--, I mean Gabriel. Do not be afraid, Mary.

Mamtha: Behold, I am the handmaiden of the Lord

Priya: (offstage) BAAAA.

Manoj: I am Gabriel, Mary, and I couldn't hear you because of the sheep.

Raj: And there were shepherds in the field, keeping watch over their flock by night.

Priya: (enters) Woof! Meow! Moo! Whatever. (everyone laughs; Mamtha enters, starts dragging Priya off). And a partridge in a pear tree (they exit)

Raj: And there were shepherds in the field, keeping watch over their flock by night. (pause) Psst. Flock!

Bara: BAAAAA (he exits, we hear dance music)

Laxman (side of mouth to Raj): **So far this has been a good Christmas play, Raj. Ed Sullivan would have liked this. When does your sister come on?**

Raj (side of mouth to Laxman): **Right after the dancing sheep, she steps out and says, 'Hark.' Then Harold Angel sings.**

Laxman (side of mouth, glancing at Raj): **Harold Angel?**

Raj (shrugs, side of mouth to Laxman) **All I know is what she told me.**

Laxman (side of mouth to Raj): **Ah, now the sheep are through dancing, Raj. Here comes your sister!**

Shanti: (enters) **Hockey stick!**

Laxman and Raj: Hockey stick? (everyone laughs, she runs off, head in hands).

Anita: And in that region there were shepherds out in the field, keeping watch over their flock by night. And an angel of the Lord appeared to them, and the glory of the Lord shone around them, and they were filled with fear. And the angel said to them, Be not afraid, for behold, I bring you good news of a great joy which will come to all the people. For to you is born this day in the city of David a Savior, who is Christ the Lord. And this will be a sign for you. You will find a babe wrapped in swaddling cloths and lying in a manger. And suddenly, there was with the angel a multitude of the heavenly host praising God and saying, Glory to God in the highest, and earth peace among men with whom he is pleased. That's what Christmas is about.

Manoj: That's right.

Laxman: So who needs Santa Claus?

Anita: And now for our closing poem. (all enter, stand in line facing audience)

Mamtha: We are here to tell you of a wondrous light.

Laxman: (whispering) **I'm sunk.**

Manoj: A wondrous light that was a star.

Laxman: (whispering) **I wonder if there's any way I could get out of here.**

Lalita: The wise men saw the star and followed it from afar.

Laxman: (whispering) **Psst, Lalita.**

Raj: They found the stable in the night beneath the star so big and bright.

Lalita: (whispering) **What's the matter.**

Laxman: (whispering) **I can't remember my piece.**

Anita: The wise men left the presents there, gifts to precious and so rare.

Lalita: (whispering) **What do you mean, you can't remember it?**

Laxman: (whispering) **I can't remember it.**

Bara: Look up! Look up! The star still stands, seen by many in many lands.

Lalita: (whispering) **You better remember it right now, or when we get home, I'll beat you.**

Laxman: THE STAR THAT SHONE AT BETHLEHEM STILL SHINES FOR US TODAY! (crumbles to floor)

Lalita: (whispering) **Merry Christmas.**

Laxman: (moaning) **Thank you.**

Act 7   Post

<u>Scene 1: Raj's house</u>

Shanti: I said hockey stick. Why, why, why? All I had to do was say hark. I ruined the whole Christmas play. Everybody hates me. Moses hates me, Luke hates me. The apostles hate me. ALL FIFTY OF THEM!

Raj: (on phone) She gets everything mixed up. She even thought someone named Harold Angel was going to sing. Excuse me, somebody's at the door (opens door).

Laxman: Hi, is Shanti home? My name is Harold Angel.

Raj: Come in, Lalita and Laxman, Anita and Manoj (they enter)

Raj and Anita: Guess what I got for Christmas? (talking at same time)
　　Raj: I got a sled and a puzzle and skates...
　　Anita: I got a doll and crayons and candy and...
Raj and Anita: What did you say?

Manoj: You got a lot of new toys.

Raj: Yes, every Christmas it's the same. The new toys come and the old toys go. That's the balance of nature. What did you get?

Manoj: A new statue of Ravi Shankar, a new Ravi Shankar sweat shirt, a Ravi Shankar ball-point pen. A twelve-volume biography of Ravi Shankar in comic-book form, and a year's supply of Ravi Shankar bubble gum. And a toy train. What will I do with a toy train?

Raj: (to Laxman) What did you get?

Laxman: Lots of things. A new bicycle, a CD player, some money, some gloves, a scout knife, a jacket, a mystery game, some puzzles, four shirts, candy and a toy car. And you know what else I got? GUILT FEELINGS, THAT'S

WHAT I GOT! This is terrible! This is my worst Christmas yet. How will I develop any character? I ALWAYS GET EVERYTHING I WANT! Anyway, now I'll write thank you notes. (he sits down, starts writing) **Dear Grandpa and Grandma.**

Lalita: (to Raj) **For three months I counted the days until Christmas. Then last week I started to count the hours. Then last night I started to count the minutes, then the seconds. I counted every second until Christmas. AND NOW IT'S ALL OVER!** (suddenly looks over at Laxman) **What are you doing?**

Laxman: Thank you for the Christmas present.

Lalita: Are you trying to make me look bad?

Laxman: I was real happy to get the fifty rupees.

Lalita: You're writing a thank-you note right away just to make me look bad, aren't you?

Laxman: It was very thoughtful of you.

Lalita: Your kind drives me crazy! Why do you have to be so efficient? Why do you have to...

Laxman: Lalita enjoyed her gift, too, and says to thank you very much. Love, Laxman.

Lalita: If you'll wait a minute, I'll run and get you a stamp (she exits)

Raj: Dear Grandma, Thank you for the nice Christmas presents. Everyone in our family liked their gifts. Even my bandar. He says to thank you for the monkey wrench.

Shanti: Dear Gramma. Thank you very much for the nice Christmas present. It was just what I wanted. What was it? (to Raj) **What did Gramma give me for Christmas?**

Raj: Which grandma? You have two.

Shanti: Any grandma! I know! Which gramma gave me the book for Christmas? The fat one or the skinny one?

Raj: The skinny one.

Shanti: Grammas should have names like people. (to Raj) And what are you going to buy with the money you got from Grandpa for Christmas.

Raj: I thought maybe I'd use it to buy a book.

Shanti: A WHAT? And now to the fat gramma. Dear Grandma, Thank you for the money you sent me for Christmas. I am going to save it for my college education. (to Raj) It's hard to write with a straight face.

Raj: I never said a word. But you spent all the money already.

Shanti: (writing) Everyone says the sweater looks good on me. Now for my other Grandma. Dear Grandma. Thank you for the pretty doll you sent me. (to Raj) Christmas thank you letters are important. They should always be written promptly. (writing) Too bad the doll fell in the river.

Raj: And with feeling.

Shanti: Of course. How about Grandpa?

Raj: Which Grandpa? You have two.

Shanti: What did I get from my aunt? Maybe I'll write to my aunt.

Raj: Which aunt? You have five.

Shanti: What did I get from my third cousin once-removed? By the way, thanks for the Christmas present.

Raj: You're welcome. I'm glad you like it.

Shanti: I didn't say I like it. What is it?

Raj: It's a game.

Shanti: I hate games.

Raj: Well, give it to someone.

Shanti: If you want it, I'll sell it to you.

Laxman: I thought maybe I'd get a monkey for Christmas, but I didn't.

Raj: Owning a monkey is a big responsibility. They need lots of care. (Bara comes and hugs him). And lots of comforting.

Laxman: We had a very traditional Christmas this year. Everything but the roasted chestnuts.

Raj: That wasn't traditional?

Laxman: Not in a microwave oven.

Raj: I just remembered something. We're supposed to read *Gulliver's Travels* during Christmas holidays and write a report on it, Anita. Have you started yet?

Anita: Started? I did mine right away so I wouldn't have to worry about it during holidays.

Raj: I hate your kind!

Anita: Thanks. Merry Christmas to you, too (she exits)

Raj: Christmas vacation will soon be over and I still haven't written my book report on *Gulliver's Travels.* I haven't even started to read it yet. Why don't I get started? Why do I put things off? (turns TV on) What's wrong with me? (pause) I just remembered. Poor Bara. He'll never know the joy of waking up on Christmas morning and finding a new bicycle for a Christmas gift. I'd

better go out and console him. (opens door, Bara comes in riding bicycle, rides around).

Shanti: (to Raj) **Is that the scarf you got for Christmas? It's kind of long, isn't it?**

Raj: A long scarf can be very useful. (he whips it around Bara's neck, brings him down, ties one end around Bara's neck, the other around his own, to Lalita) **Now that Christmas programs are over, I hear the panchayat is planning a New Year's program. They need a little boy to play the part of the new year.**

Laxman: Boy, I sure pity that poor kid whoever he is.

Lalita: (smiling to Laxman) **Haven't you heard?**

Laxman: OH NO! (shields face in hands).

Raj: (to Lalita) **It's your fault, you know. First you volunteered him for the panchayat Christmas program, and when he survived that, for the CHURCH Christmas program, and when he survived THAT, you turned right around and volunteered him for the New Year's program. It's your fault he's upset. Can't you at least say something to him?**

Lalita: (to Laxman) **Chicken!**

Scene 2: Lalita's house

Lalita: Everything is hopeless. What's the use? Nobody cares.

Laxman: I hate to say this, but you've been very crabby since Christmas.

Lalita: Anyone who is at all sensitive is bound to have a post-Christmas letdown. I have it regularly. A deep depression sets in. Your bones ache. You feel tired all

over. And if anyone even mentions 'partridge in a pear tree,' you want to scream.

Laxman: Partridge in a pear tree.

Lalita: AAAAAUGH

Laxman: Isn't being crabby and having a post-Christmas letdown really the same thing?

Lalita: NOT AT ALL! (knock on door)

Laxman: Come in, Manoj and Anita, Raj and Bara. (they enter)

Lalita: Manoj, I just wanted to thank you again for the string of pearls you gave me for Christmas.

Manoj: I did not give you a string of pearls for Christmas.

Lalita: YOU SURE DIDN'T! At least I thank you for the mink stole you gave me for Christmas.

Manoj: I didn't give you a mink stole for Christmas, either.

Lalita: THAT'S RIGHT! Well, would you be offended if I exchanged the present you gave me for Christmas?

Manoj: I didn't give you ANY present for Christmas.

Lalita: AND DON'T THINK I DIDN'T NOTICE!

Shanti: And don't anyone talk to me. I'm having my post-Christmas letdown.

Raj: I just wanted to thank you again for the wonderful present you gave me. It was just what I wanted.

Shanti: Why do you always have to say something nice?

Lalita: Manoj, what's a sure cure for Post-Christmas letdown?

Raj: Pat a monkey on the head. (she pats Bara on the head, walks away to get jacket)

Bara: And how do I cure MY post-Christmas let-down? My brother gave me a tie for Christmas. I suppose he'll be hurt if I don't wear it at least once. I think he painted the peacock on it himself. (door knock)

Raj: Hi, Priya. Enter. (she enters)

Priya: Hi, Raj. Did your monkey get that Christmas sweater I knit for him? Oh, there he is.

Raj: Yes, thank you very much. He likes it. He is wildly enthusiastic.

Bara: Yeah, right.

Shanti: (to Bara) **Ahem. I see you're not wearing my Christmas present. I bought it for you with my own money. If a person goes out of her way to buy you something special, the least you can do is wear it.**

Bara: All right, I'll wear it. I'll wear it! But it's not the sort of thing you wear every day. Besides, I was saving it in case I got invited to Scotland for golf. (puts on hat)

Lalita: (re-enters) **Guess where I'm going, Raj? My mother is taking me downtown to see all the Christmas decorations.**

Raj: You're too late. They're starting to put things up for Republic Day. And thanks for the Christmas card you sent me.

Lalita: I never sent you any Christmas card.

Raj: Don't know sarcasm when you hear it?

Anita: I'm so sorry you didn't get a Christmas card.

Raj: Oh, I finally got one, all right. I'm the only person I know who had to go out and buy himself a Christmas card! I don't understand it. How come some people get no Christmas cards while other people get a whole lot of them?

Bara: Some of us have more friends.

Raj: Since Christmas is all over and I didn't get a single Christmas card, I know nobody likes me.

Anita: Don't forget, Raj, that when people send cards to your mom and dad, they mean to include you.

Raj: That's true. Thanks.

Priya: No one sent me a Christmas card, either.

Raj: Did you send any yourself?

Priya: Did I what?

Raj: (to Laxman) **Where's your Christmas tree?**

Laxman: All the decorations and ornaments have been packed away, and everything cleaned up. How about you?

Priya: I haven't sent out my Christmas cards yet.

Shanti: And Christmas is over, but Bara is still celebrating. What could be later than that?

Priya: Happy Divali!

Scene 3: Raj's house

Raj: I didn't get one Christmas card, not one. Oh well, what' the use of thinking about it? Sleep is the only real cure for discouragement. You just have to go to sleep and try to forget everything, and... (pause, suddenly sits up) **NOT ONE!**

Scene 4: Shop

Bara: (sticks his tongue out) **Bleah. Every time we have a New Year party, I drink too much coke.**

Raj: Memsahib, my monkey wants to return this book he got for Christmas. He doesn't like it because the hero is a leopard. He hates leopards.

Bara: Bleah!

Raj: He wants a book where all the leopards get eaten by alligators on the first page. (Bara is smiling). And **I'd like to return something I bought here.**

Laxman: It's a Christmas present for a girl, but he was too shy to give it to her.

Raj: It was never opened. Yes, I was going to give it to the little Punjabi girl in our class.

Laxman: You know her?

Raj: You're her Mom? You work here in this store?

Laxman: When we first saw you, we thought you were her older sister. (they exit)

Raj: Why did you tell her that?

Laxman: She let you return the present, didn't she?

Scene 5: Back to School

Priya: Weren't we supposed to read a book or something during Christmas vacation?

Mamtha: A book. *Hans Brinker.*

Priya: What's it about?

Mamtha: It's about this kid who skates.

Priya: Ice or rollerblade? (to teacher) **I got a simple pass for the whole last semester? Memsahib, I'm very hurt. I think I deserved a better mark. Oh, by the way, while we're talking. Here's the book report that was due last month. And today's Christmas reading report?** (stands in front, to class) **Christmas Holiday Reading Report. Reading is one of my favorite pastimes.**

Mamtha: I can't stand to listen to this.

Priya: And I read every day. And you know what I read? A comic book!

Mamtha: AAAAUGH. (Priya goes back to her desk)

Priya: (to Manoj) **The teacher stuck a gold star on your paper! She never sticks a star on any of my papers. I COULDN'T GET A STAR ON A CHRISTMAS TREE! Sorry, memsahib.** (to Mamtha) **Mamtha, what did you write for the essay on how you spent your Christmas holiday?**

Mamtha: I wrote about how I visited the museum, and cleaned out our garage and helped Mom polish all the silverware.

Priya: I hate your kind, Mamtha. (she starts writing) **How I Spent My Christmas Holiday. Worrying about this assignment.** (she crumples up the paper, starts again). **What I did on my Christmas holiday. I went outside and looked at the clouds. They formed beautiful patterns with beautiful colors. I looked at them every morning and every evening. Which is all I did on my Christmas holiday. And what's wrong with that?**

Laxman: Hi, Mamtha. I thought about you a lot during Christmas holidays. Thank you for the nice Christmas card. I really wanted to send you one, too, you know. I still can't figure out why you wouldn't give me your address.

Mamtha: Today my name is Mother Theresa.

Laxman: Did you miss me during Christmas holidays?

Mamtha: Did you give me a Christmas present?

Laxman: No.

Mamtha: I didn't miss you.

Scene 6: Outdoors

Laxman: What grade did you get on your book report, Raj?

Raj: Simple pass. As low as you can get without failing. The teacher said it looked like the sort of report that was written after midnight on the last day of Christmas holiday. What could I say? I congratulated her on her remarkable perceptivity.

Mamtha: (enters, running) You won, Priya.

Priya: Won what?

Mamtha: They just made an announcement. (Bara enters) Our classmate, Priya's, essay on 'What you did during Christmas holidays' won the 'all city school essay contest'. First prize! Congratulations. (Priya starts to cry). Don't wipe your tears away with your French fries, Priya.

Priya: How did I win? I got a simple pass. (to Raj) Explain this, if you can. Everyone in the class writes an essay. I get mine back with simple pass. All those essays go to the city essay contest, and I won. Explain. (they shrug, exit)

Bara: (to audience) **I'll explain: Never listen to the reviewers.**

Scene 7: School
Priya (the microphone is too low, so Mamtha is picking up Priya to speak)**: I've been asked to read the essay I wrote about my Christmas holidays. Perhaps, however, a few words might be in order to tell—**

Mamtha: Hurry up and read it!

Priya: Mamtha!

Scene 8: Outdoors

Shanti: Have you thought about what you're going to get me for Christmas?

Raj: We just HAD Christmas!

Shanti: It'll be here again before you know it.

Raj: Remember, if we meet someone on the sidewalk, say 'Happy New Year.'

Shanti: If I say, 'Happy New Year,' will they give me a bicycle.

Lalita: No, they won't give you anything.

Shanti: Let's go home.

Raj: Christmas is over, but I still feel joyful. I think I'll keep this good feeling about myself and everyone for a long time. Why only this time of year? Why not all year 'round?

Lalita: Who cares? What are you, some kind of fanatic or something?

Raj: And a happy new year to you, too!

Anita: Do you realize there are only 347 days until Christmas?

Lalita: Don't I know it! And New Year's comes right after that. If just doesn't seem possible.

Anita: I don't know where the time goes.

HOW TO DO A CHRISTMAS PROGRAM

By Stanley Scism

At Scism Christian Institute, our favorite Christmas programs have been several days long, yet easy to do because they involve a lot of prepared materials and minimum memorization. To do this, you must of course prepare materials in advance.

First, we gather as many materials as we can from many varied sources. This gives us much stuff to brainstorm with. We have Christmas videos, CDs, cassettes, books, plays, magazine articles and drama scripts collected from past efforts. Don't throw away records of your past productions and activities—they might work well with a different audience, or they might work well with parts of each program combined to form a new whole. (You get different audiences if you go on the road, or if you bring a program to a different age group. You can even use the same script if you have a group of people who really liked the original performance and want to try doing it themselves. The question then becomes who they'll do it for, since your original audience has already seen it. If it was really good, they might want to see it again. And even if it wasn't originally that outstanding so as to demand an encore, you can perform it at another venue. At the college, we can rotate programs through as soon as the freshman class at the last one graduates. BA programs in India are three years long, so we can recycle programs as they are, with small updates every three years.

You can also alter a program and make it fresh even for the same audience—one humorous way being by spoofs, parodies, pastiche. A straightforward way to do this is simply a retelling of a story from another perspective. For instance, I wrote a drama of the Christmas story from Joseph's perspective. A lady who has been through pregnancy and childbearing might be able to write one from Mary's.

Here's what we did for various programs:

A. Christmas Eve EVE Fa-La-La

79

This December 23 evening emphasizes music and decoration—a sort of kickoff for Christmas celebration. We sang songs about Christmas decorations—an obvious one would be 'Deck the Halls,' you can also add 'The Holly and the Ivy.' On Christmas music, there are many—'Ding! Dong! Merrily On High,' 'Patapan,' 'Little Drummer Boy,' 'There's a Song In the Air,' 'Let Our Gladness Know No End' and 'Here We Come A-Caroling.' We sang them in this order so we would start with the lightest, get more serious in message, and finish with a flourish.

Then we saw a Christmas concert video by Jose Carreras, Natalie Cole and Placido Domingo. Obviously, if we had live singers who were really good, that would be better, but a good Christmas concert on video is better than an awful one in person.

We finished with coffee punch. Yes!

B. Christmas Eve

This December 24 evening emphasizes the humorous, light side of Christmas. Those of you severe people who feel that Christmas is being trivialized and who want to solve that by eradicating it completely, please remember that Oliver Cromwell and company tried that. It doesn't work. People got tired of heaviness all the time and they went back to frivolity with a vengeance—the Restoration under Charles II was far more immoral than the original problem under Charles I had ever been. Therefore, the best solution is probably to separate the frolic and froth from the true, deep, real meaning, have one evening for the one and the other evening for the other. We have Christmas eve for humor and Santa and gifts for each other, and Christmas day for the real, deep, particular meaning behind this festival.

With this plan, we on December 24 in some years start with our own version of 'Twelve Days of Christmas,' 'being a most cunningly devised alteration of the original script' that involves students singing particular days with gifts chosen according to their interests. For instance, one year, for the first day of Christmas, two guitar enthusiasts sing that they'd received 'a top-flight new guitar,' and on the second day, three electronics whizzes sing that they'd received 'a brand new battery tester.' Married students away from their families sing that on the fifth day of Christmas they received 'A TICKET HOME TO MY WIIIIIIFE.' You get the idea.

Once I did a version of "'Twas the Night Before Christmas,' accompanied on tom-toms by my secretary. Then someone else did 'The Gospel According to a Sheep.' I read to the students O Henry's story, 'The Gift of the Magi.' We saw the video *Muppet Christmas Carol* (a spoof of Dickens' *Christmas Carol,* which we had seen the previous year and acted in a previous year). We all ate fudge cake and exchanged gifts.

Another year, we sang parodies of a number of Christmas songs: 'Angelic College Students Singing O'er the Plains,' 'Away In a Hostel,' 'Come, Thou Long-awaited Commencement,' and 'The First Train West' (to the tune of 'The First Noel.') We saw the video 'Miracle on Thirty-Fourth Street,' enjoyed banana pudding, and I gave a very short Christmas speech adapted from Mr. Pickwick's in Charles Dickens' *Pickwick Papers.* One of our youth groups put on a short Christmas drama, I read them a short story, and we closed in prayer. People who still didn't want to go to sleep stayed up and sang all night long, knowing they still had to be alert and in place for the December 25 AM program.

Christmas morning, churches have church services and these involve music or drama programs. One year we had a narrator between songs, but that isn't as good as having drama or songs themselves carry the story forward. If you have a multi-cultural group, however, who know Christmas songs from their various backgrounds, you can announce sufficiently in advance to allow for practices and auditions, then at audition put your program together, assemble it in order, inform all participating parties of the sequence of events, and have a dress rehearsal. Make sure the songs are not all by the same kind of group (not all choirs, not all trios, not all solos, for instance) or the same kind of music. Variety, variety.

If you decide not to go multilingual or multicultural routes, or if you simply don't have the people to do that, you can still have songs, even very familiar ones, carry the story along. Don't sing ALL the verses of ALL the songs—several songs cover the whole Christmas story, so you'd be going back and forth over the same material. We started with verse one of 'O Come, O Come Emmanuel' (you could use 'Come, Thou Long Expected Jesus' for this instead, but 'O Come, O Come' has a minor key, wistful sound appropriate to people waiting sadly and longing for the Messiah. If you want something more upbeat, go with 'Come, Thou Long-Expected.')

After that, we went to the scene of Mary at home, when Gabriel speaks to her. Then comes 'O Come, O Come,' verse 4, then the scene of Joseph at home, having consulted the priest and now being told in a dream to marry Mary. Then came 'O Little Town of Bethlehem,' verse 1, sung while Mary and Joseph travel. At Bethlehem, they search for a room, (the carol 'No Room', verse 1, fits here), end up in the stable, after which 'O Little Town,' verses 2 and 3 were sung, and then immediately a soloist rendered 'O Holy Night.' 'O Holy Night' is *made* for a soloist. If you don't have one, you can skip the song or use a group, but whoever sings it should do so energetically.

Now come the shepherds and angels, the choir sings, *with the congregation* (the music program contains words to all songs in which the congregation participates), 'Hark! The Herald Angels Sing,' verses 1 and 2. The shepherds arrive at the manger, after which choir and congregation sing 'Silent Night.' The choir sings 'Angels We Have Heard,' verses 1 and 3.

Finally, here come the wise men, who also sing the trio 'We Three Kings,' verses 2, 3 and 4. Then the choir and congregation join them singing verses 1, 5 and chorus after each verse (this is a slightly different arrangement, but you can indicate it on your program sheet, your congregation can understand it—this isn't rocket science.)

Choir and congregation then sing 'O Come, All Ye Faithful,' verses 1-3 and 'Joy To the World,' verses 1 and 2. This whole Christmas morning pageant takes 30 minutes, maybe 45.

Another time, we had a regular play, interrupted at intervals by songs in various languages that fit that particular part of the program. We also had sheep singing 'Go Tell It On the Mountain' and camels dancing and playing the mandolin and guitar. It was wonderful. Christmas morning each year, the program tells the story, by either music or drama, not by sermons—the people have received Christmas sermons in mid-December already. The ministers can hardly ignore Christmas until Christmas day because it dominates the culture and economy long before the actual day arrives.

I'm very open to new dramas that involve audience participation and then invite people to give their lives to and live their lives for Jesus Christ.

Christmas evening, we cut past all peripherals and sing songs about Jesus birth itself—the great meaning of this celebration: 'I Heard the Bells,' 'Coventry Carol,' 'Redeeming Love,' 'What Child Is This?' 'Silent Night,' and 'O Holy Night.' And we watch tape one of the famous video *Jesus of Nazareth*. Afterward, we ate something not too heavy, but also not just a sweet, since we'd eaten Christmas dinner in mid-afternoon.

If you have to scope your whole program down to one evening and can't do all these different programs on different nights, I suggest having the audition, then making the program, scheduling lighter events earlier in the program, moving to serious events and deeper meaning as you go along. One year, we had a marching band from one youth group march and play 'Good Christian Men, Rejoice,' a youth comedy group do a comical music routine, and a youth drama group put on a serious skit. All that together took 30 minutes. We had refreshments, sang multicultural Christmas songs from various language areas, closed with the *Jesus of Nazareth* video. If you don't want to do video and have only the one night, you can have your live drama instead. The whole evening would not take more than 90 minutes.

One more thing: build up these events in advance by raising Christmas consciousness. From magazines you can find well-presented articles, poems, recipes, thoughts, comedy, stories, and so on and on for your bulletin board. And if you keep these on file, you'll have them for future years in case supplies and/or time run low. I typed up a series of Christmas readings I can use for bulletin boards, programs, magazines, handouts, or performances.

If you don't want to creatively put anything together, the market has enough cantatas to gag a goat. Musicians produce them every year, but look through them before you buy. If the cantata is heavy on unfamiliar songs, look more closely. It's a vehicle to advertise the writer's new songs, and you need to detect whether they're good or not. Find or compile a cantata that has a few new songs and a lot of favorites. People like hearing old songs in new arrangements sometimes, though not, of course, if they're expected to sing along. Then you'd have confusion, unless your audience knows the music well. Special-song new arrangements updating golden oldies, plus a few sing-along ones in standard arrangements, plus two or a few brand new songs, will probably satisfy a lot of people. Choose new songs good enough to incorporate into worship or future programs—otherwise they are just left dangling and forgotten. You can combine cantatas—these songs or scripts from this one, those songs or scripts from another. Make yours the best—pick the cream from each crop.

God bless. Enjoy your holiday. Don't run yourself ragged with these. Involve as many people as possible, each doing the part—decorations, singing, drama, cooking—that they like best. You can all have a wonderful holiday together.

Stanley Scism writes books, articles, college lectures, songs, poems and other things he might have forgotten just now. He founded, presides over and teaches occasionally in Scism Christian University's campuses. He founded and leads Yesu Mandali in Nepal, Yesu Kalishia in India, and Stanley Society in India. He founded Wonderful Words publishing, Light and Life music ministry, Head & Heart Ministers' Meetings. He enjoys his friends in the USA, UK, Republic of Ireland, India, Nepal and in nations he doesn't get to visit regularly.

His books are, in order of publication:

Lera, a biography of a minister from Manipur, who also lived many years in Meghalaya, who baptized over 6000 people, started over 50 churches, opened up three whole new areas to the message.

Little Lady, a biography of a lady from Arunachal Pradesh, who endured horrible privations as a child, found relief and rescue in Jesus Christ, has told many of her home people about Him.

Northwest Passage, volume one of the biography of Ellis Scism, who grew up in Oregon, went to college in California, pastored churches in Washington and Idaho, led a group of ministers from Alaska to Wyoming—all this before going to India as a founding missionary.

A Look at Revelation, James Stewart's teaching on the Biblical book, rendered into writing by Stanley Scism

Baptism, a pocket-sized study.

Stanley Scism's Songs!, his lyrics to his and other people's melodies.

Devoted, sixty short meditations for public or personal devotions.

Praying Heart, 13 meditations on devotion and communion for one quarter of the year.

Big Blue Songbook: Sigma Songbook, 9th edition. Compiled by Stanley Scism for SCI-New Delhi.

Do You Hear What I Hear?, 3rd edition. Christmas songbook compiled by Stanley Scism for SCI-New Delhi.

Tell Me About Your Life, by Katy Collins (mostly) and Stanley Scism (a little bit). An overview of the Bible through Bible characters, for children's ministry

Pacific Patrol. Dale Short's diary of navy service in Iwo Jima, Okinawa and other places during WW2.

A Himalayan Christmas, a drama of the year's highest point, set in the world's highest place.

A Look at Spiritual Gifts, James Stewart's teaching on gifts of the Spirit, rendered into writing by Stanley Scism.

India Calling. Ellis Scism's autobiography of his founding of a new apostolic church group in India. Republished by Wonderful Words.